POEMS

FROM MANY CULTURES

Published by
Evans Brothers Limited
2A Portman Mansions
Chiltern Street
London W1U 6NR

© Evans Brothers Limited 2001

First published in 2001

Printed in Hong Kong by Wing King Tong Co. Ltd

British Library Cataloguing in Publication Data
Poems from many cultures
    1. Poetry – Collections
    I. Waters, Fiona
    808.8'1

    ISBN 0237521040

Editor: Su Swallow
Design: Simon Borrough
Production: Jenny Mulvanny

Picture acknowledgements
Page 7 Bruce Coleman
Page 23 Robert Harding
Page 33 AKG London
Page 34 Superstock
Page 49 Trip/H Rogers
Page 51 Trip/W Jacobs
Page 53 Trip/J Highet
Page 60 Trip/H Rogers
Page 72 B&C Alexander
Page 84 Bruce Coleman
Page 92 Mary Evans Picture Library
Page 96 The Bridgeman Art Library
Additional images by Jon Swallow, Simon Borrough and
Bethany Borrough

With love to Verna who opened my eyes

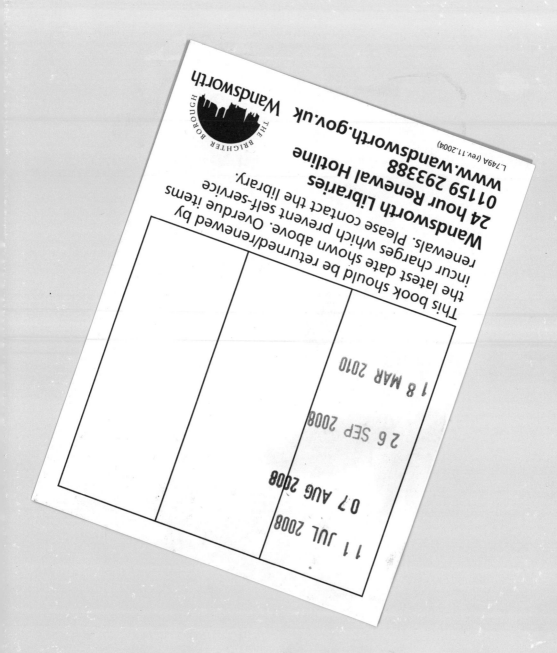

Wandsworth
THE BRIGHTER BOROUGH

L.749A (rev.11.2004)
www.wandsworth.gov.uk
01159 293388
24 hour Renewal Hotline
Wandsworth Libraries

This book should be returned/renewed by
the latest date shown above. Overdue items
incur charges which prevent self-service
renewals. Please contact the library.

18 MAR 2010

26 SEP 2008

0 7 AUG 2008

11 JUL 2008

POEMS FROM MANY CULTURES

Poetry Collection 4

Compiled by Fiona Waters

Evans

EVANS BROTHERS LIMITED

Contents

The Door

Miroslav Holub (Czechoslovakia)

Go and open the door.
    Maybe outside there's
    a tree, or a wood,
    a garden,
    or a magic city.

Go and open the door.
    Maybe a dog's rummaging.
    Maybe you'll see a face,
or an eye,
or the picture
      of a picture.

Go and open the door.
    If there's a fog
    it will clear.

Go and open the door.
    Even if there's only
    the darkness ticking,
    even if there's only
    the hollow wind,
    even if
      nothing
        is there,
go and open the door.

At least
there'll be
a draught.

The First Rule of Sinhalese Architecture

Michael Ondaatje (Sri Lanka)

Never build three doors
in a straight line

A devil might rush
through them
deep into your house,
into your life

The Guardians

George Mackay Brown (Scotland)

May a strong guardian
Stand at the door
With sword and olive branch.

May the keeper of the windows
Be eager-eyed
For dawn and first star,
    snow-light and corn-light.

May the keeper of the fire
See a loaf on the table
And faces of travellers lit with welcome
    and shadow-of-flame, in winter.

May the keeper of the beds be resolute
Against the terror that walks by night,
And herd with gentleness the flocks of sleep.

In a blue-and-silver morning
On the first winter step
Those guardians, and others who hold
    a finger to the lip, smiling
Came about her who holds now the key of the house.

The Wee Malkies

Stephen Mulrine *(Scotland)*

Whit'll ye dae when the wee Malkies come,
if they dreep doon affy the wash-hoose dyke
an' pit the hems oan the sterrheid light,
an' play keepie-up oan the clean close-wa',
an blooter yir windae in wi' the ba',
   missis, whit'll ye dae?

Whit'll ye dae when the wee malkies come,
if they chap yir door an' choke the drains,
an' caw the feet fae yir sapsy weans,
an' tummle thur wulkies through yir sheets,
an' tim thur chanties oot in the street,
   missis, whit'll ye dae?

Whit'll ye dae when the wee Malkies come,
if they chuck thur screwtaps doon the pan,
an' stick the heid oan the sanit'ry man;
when ye hear thum schauchlin' doon yir loaby,
shoutin', 'WEE MALKIES! The gemme's . . . a bogey!'
   Hey, missis, whit'll ye dae?

Inside My Zulu Hut

Oswald Mbuyiseni Mtshali (South Africa)

It is a hive
without any bees
to build the walls
with golden bricks of honey.
A cave cluttered
with a millstone,
calabashes of sour milk
claypots of foaming beer
sleeping grass mats
wooden head rests
tanned goat skins
tied with riempies
to wattle rafters
blackened by the smoke
of kneaded cow dung
burning under
the three-legged pot
on the earthen floor
to cook my porridge.

Evening Darkens

Anonymous (Japan)

Evening darkens until
I can no longer see the path.
Still I find my way home,
My horse has gone this way
before.

The Earth And The People

Traditional (*Inuit*)

The earth was here before the people.
The very first people
came out of the ground.
Everything came from the ground,
even caribou.
Children once grew
out of the ground
just as flowers do.
Women out wandering
found them sprawling on the grass
and took them home and nursed them.
That way people multiplied.

This land of ours
has become habitable
because we came here
and learned how to hunt.

The Small Window

RS Thomas *(Wales)*

In Wales there are jewels
To gather, but with the eye
Only. A hill lights up
Suddenly; a field trembles
With colour and goes out
In its turn; in one day
You can witness the extent
Of the spectrum and grow rich

With looking. Have a care;
This wealth is for the few
And chosen. Those who crowd
A small window dirty it
With their breathing, though sublime
And inexhaustible the view.

My Garden

Redmond Phillips (Australia)

at school every child has
a little garden
it was miss frohms idea
and the best garden gets a certificate
ernie mcwhidden is doing well
with beetroot and iceland poppies
pamela greavey
has violets and pansies
everybody is growing the usual things
in the usual way

but i
i have strange exotic plants
from far off lands
as far apart as tamarisk and cammeray
golden snaggletuft
maidens mole
climbing spittlecress
a border of prinkulas waffleberries
and sky blue daisies
the hardy brassicas
fragile tittiplipsias from nijni novgorod
great horned ramflowers
and goonias everywhere
then my proud boast
mrs hubert mcgillicuddy
which is
a rose

it was also miss frohms idea
that i should write out
a garden is a lovesome thing god wot
one hundred times
how foolish of me to name a large
clump of stinkweed
frohmia

Spirit Belong Mother

Eva Johnson (Aboriginal)

I not see you long time now, I not see you long time now,
White fella bin take me from you, I don't know why
Give me to missionary to be God's child
Give me new language, give me new name
All time I cry, they say - that shame
I go to city down south, real cold
I forget all your stories, my mother you told
Gone is my spirit, my dreaming, my name
Gone to these people, our country to claim
They gave me white mother, she give me new name
All time I cry, she say - that shame,
I not see you long time now, I not see you long time now.

I grow as woman now, not piccaninny no more
I need you to teach me your wisdom, your lore
I am your spirit, I'll stay alive
But in white fella way, you won't survive

I'll fight for your land, for your sacred sites
To sing and to dance with the brolga in flight
To continue to live in your own tradition -
A culture for me was replaced by a mission
I not see you long time now, I not see you long time now.

One day your dancing your dreaming your song
Will take me your spirit back where I belong
My mother the earth, the land, I demand
Protection from aliens who rule, who command
For they do not know where our dreaming began
Our destiny lies in the laws of white man
   Two women we stand, our story untold
      But now as our spiritual bondage unfold
         We will silence this burden, this longing, this pain
         When I hear you my mother, give me my name
         I not see you long time now, I not see you long time now.

Prayer

Imtiaz Dharker (Pakistan)

The place is full of worshippers.
You can tell by the sandals
piled outside, the owners' prints
worn into leather, rubber, plastic,
a picture clearer than their faces
put together, with some originality,
brows and eyes, the slant
of cheek to chin.

What prayer are they whispering?
Each one has left a mark,
the perfect pattern of a need,
sole and heel and toe
in dark curved patches,
heels worn down,
thongs ragged, mended many times.
So many shuffling hopes,
pounded into print,
as clear as the pages of holy books,
illuminated with the glint
of gold around the lettering.

What are they whispering?
Outside, in the sun,
such a quiet crowd
of shoes, thrown together
like a thousand prayers
washing against the walls of God.

The Convict And The Lady

James McAuley (Australia)

An incident in St George's Church, Battery Point

Voluntaries of Clarke and Boyce
    Flow temperately sweet
With Gamba, Flute and Clarabel
And pedal Bourdon trampled well
    By shapely kid-skinned feet.

An apparition from the tower
    Suspends the diapason.
Will she scream? No, courage wins,
And in that empty church begins
    An interesting liaison.

'Lady, I am a fugitive
    That's taken refuge here.
Up into the tower I crept,
Two days and nights I've waked and slept,
    But hunger masters fear.

'Now fetch me food, or fetch the law,
    For I am at your mercy.
Though forfeited in youthful spleen,
My birth and station were not mean,
    My name is Eustace Percy.'

So every day she brings her lunch,
  And practises the organ.
She finds him breeches, coat and vest,
And takes word to The Sailor's Rest,
  To a man named Harry Morgan.

One Sunday, as the lady plays
  'Recessional in A',
A stranger joins the genteel throng
That files out after Evensong;
  Unmarked, he slips away.

In darkness a small boat rows out
  Into the estuary.
The brig looms up upon the tide,
A shadow clambers up the side -
  And Eustace Percy's free!

So ends the tale? No, three years passed;
  From Hull a letter came:
'I thrive in my new way of life '
The lady sailed to be his wife,
  And shared a borrowed name.

Organist, for that lady's sake,
  Select your stops and play
This postlude that I chose expressly,
By Samuel Sebastian Wesley,
  'Recessional in A'.

Two Friends

Nikki Giovanni
(Africa/America)

lydia and shirley have
two pierced ears and
two bare ones
five pigtails
two pairs of sneakers
two berets
two smiles
one necklace
one bracelet
lots of stripes and
one good friendship

Dancing Poinciana

Telcine Turner (Bahamas)

Fire in the treetops,
Fire in the sky.
Blossoms red as sunset
Dazzling to the eye.

Dance, Poinciana,
Sway, Poinciana,
On a sea of green.
Dance, Poinciana,
Regal as a queen.

Fire in the treetops,
Fire in the sky.
Crimson petals and white
Stained with scarlet dye.

Dance, Poinciana,
Sway, Poinciana,
On a sea of green.
Dance Poinciana,
Sway, Poinciana,
Regal as a queen.

Nightsong City

Dennis Brutus *(Zimbabwe)*

Sleep well, my love, sleep well:
the harbour lights glaze over restless docks,
police cars cockroach through the tunnel streets

from the shanties creaking iron-sheets
violence like a bug-infested rag is tossed
and fear is immanent as sound in the wind-swung bell;

the long day's anger pants from sand and rocks;
but for this breathing night at least,
my land, my love, sleep well.

Night

Sergei Esenin *(Russia)*

Silently sleeps the river.
The dark pines hold their peace.
The nightingale does not sing.
Or the corncrake screech.

Night. Silence enfolds.
Only the brook murmurs.
And the brilliant moon turns
Everything to silver.

Silver the river.
And the rivulets.
Silver the grass
Of the fertile steppes.

Night. Silence enfolds.
All sleeps in Nature
And the brilliant moon
Turns everything to silver.

Morning

Dionne Brand *(Trinidad)*

Day came in
on an old brown bus
with two friends.
She crept down
an empty street
bending over
to sweep the thin dawn away.
With her broom,
she drew red streaks
in the corners
of the dusty sky
and finding a rooster still asleep,
prodded him into song.
A fisherman,
not far from the shore,
lifted his eyes,
saw her coming,
and yawned.
The bus rolled by,
and the two friends caught
a glimpse of blue
as day swung around a corner
to where the sea met a road.
The sky blinked,
woke up,
and might have changed its mind,
but day had come.

Frost

Valerie Bloom *(Trinidad)*

Overnight, a giant spilt icing sugar on the ground,
He spilt it on the hedgerows, and the trees without a sound,
He made a wedding-cake of the haystack in the field,
He dredged the countryside and the grass was all concealed
He sprinkled sugar on the roofs, in patches not too neat,
And in the morning when we woke, the world around was
sweet.

Sheep

K E Ingram *(Jamaica)*

God made sheep in the early morning.

In his hands he caught the clusters
Of the fleecy clouds of dawning
And tied them in bunches
And fastened their feet and their noses
With wet brown clay.

And into their eyes he dropped
With reeds from a nearby river
The light of the dying morning star
And the light of the dying moon.

And then on that creation morning
When the sun had flooded the peaks and plains
And the dew lay thick on the rushes
Man saw sheep on the grazing grass
And heard the sadness of their bleating.

Beach

Shinkichi Takahashi (Japan)

Gale: tiles, roofs whirling,
disappearing at once.

Rocks rumble, mountains
swallow villages,
yet insects, birds chirp by
the shattered bridge.

Men shoot through space,
race sound. On TV nations
maul each other, endlessly.

Why this confusion,
how restore the ravaged
body of the world?

Time is Running Out

Oodgeroo Noonuccal *(Aboriginal)*

The miner rapes
The heart of the hearth
With his violent spade.
Stealing, bottling her black blood
For the sake of greedy trade.
On his metal throne of destruction,
He labours away with a will,
Piling the mountainous minerals high
With giant tool and iron drill.

In his greedy lust for power,
He destroys old nature's will.
For the sake of the filthy dollar,
He dirties the nest he builds.
Well he knows that violence
Of his destructive kind
Will be violently written
Upon the sands of time.

But time is running out
And time is close at hand,
For the Dreamtime folk are massing
To defend their timeless land.
Come gentle black man
Show your strength;
Time to take a stand.
Make the violent miner feel
Your violent
Love of land.

Outline

Imtiaz Dharker (Pakistan)

A solid figure struggles out of rock.
The sculptor's chisel
chose to stop
at just this moment, leaving
the body locked
in a great struggle, trembling
on the fine edge between
being trapped, and being free.

* * *

The artist tries, time after time,
to trap the human body
in a fine outline;
and finds himself, instead, cut loose,
floating free through the spaces
of the wheeling mind.

Boy on a Swing

Oswald Mbuyiseni Mtshali *(South Africa)*

Slowly he moves
to and fro, to and fro,
then faster and faster
he swishes up and down.

His blue shirt
billows in the breeze
like a tattered kite.

The world whirls by:
east becomes west,
north turns to south;
the four cardinal points
meet in his head.

      Mother!
Where did I come from?
When will I wear long trousers?
Why was my father jailed?

Martin And The Hand Grenade

John Foulcher *(Australia)*

Martin displays the grenade, the class pauses
for history. With his father's bleak skill
Martin edges out the firing pin, indicates

the chamber where the powder went; he fingers
the serrations, bristles with the shrapnel
possibilities. Questions. No - it had limited
power: ten yards, then the spread
became too loose to catch a man's mortality.
Around the class now. And each boy holds

the small war, lifts it into the air
above the desk trenches: the dead weapon hurls
across mind fields, tears the heart ahead.

1938

Pastor Niemoller (Germany)

'First they came for the Jews
And I did not speak out -
Because I was not a Jew.

Then they came for the communists
And I did not speak out -
Because I was not a communist.

Then they came for the trade unionists
And I did not speak out -
Because I was not a trade unionist.

Then they came for me -
And there was no one left
To speak out for me.'

The Bird

Adonis (Ali Ahmad Sa'id) *(Syria)*

On mount Sinnin
I heard a bird
Crying for peace.

Its songs
Cut through
The city's coldness
Like razor blades.

Only Ashes Remain

Bairam Haliti *(Croatia)*

They come from far flung places -
men, women, children,
hungry, dry, unshod -
They are the Roma,
dressed in rags,
walking through mud.

They are drawn by
promises of a land
they can call their own,
houses, fields, firesides:
false Ustashi words.

They are a people of sorrow.

Only a chamber of gas
awaits them.
Their infants are screaming,
all sleep forsaken.
Their land is a mound
of charred limbs.

Where once there were
dreams,
white horses,
distant plains,
only ashes remain.
The innocent child's smile
has evaporated into sky.

The Raid

Alexian Santino Spinelli (Italy)

A knock on the door in the deepest night
the ferocious teeth of trained dogs
an automatic gun pointed at the sleepy face
shattered dream nightmarish hallucinations
black uniforms piercing stares
disgust and hate slanderous accusations
violent hurricane innocent eyes . . .
the door closed a dream disappeared
tears on the ground . . . torn hearts.

Don't Ask Me

Jon Milos (Yugoslavia)

Don't ask me
Who won the first Marathon
I am not interested in sport

Don't ask me
Who dropped the first nuclear bomb
That is not my problem

Don't ask me
Who painted the Mona Lisa
I don't care for Art

Don't ask me
Who got the Nobel prize in literature this year
I am not paid for that

Don't ask me
Who wrote the ninth symphony
Music doesn't move me.

Don't ask me
Who first set foot on the moon
I couldn't care less.

Don't ask me
Who murdered Julius Caesar
It is no concern of mine

Don't ask me
I have no time for stupid things
I have my job to do
And my family to care for
About anything else
I don't give a damn.

Sitting On A Balcony

Charles Mungoshi
(Zimbabwe)

Sitting on the balcony
fingering a glass of beer
I have bought without
any intention to drink:
I see a little boy
poking for something
in a refuse dump:
looking for a future?
I am afraid the stars say
your road leads to another
balcony, just like this one:
where you will sit
fingering a beer you have bought
without any intention to drink.

The Moon Always Follows the Sun

Traditional *(Congo)*

Calm down, little brother,
Time heals all wounds.
No matter how much one is weeping,
The moon always follows the sun.

Eat your bananas and fresh leaves,
And don't cry any more,
Because forever and ever
The moon will follow the sun.

Lullaby

Akan *(Africa)*

Someone would like to have you for her child
but you are mine.
Someone would like to rear you on a costly mat
but you are mine.
Someone would like to place you on a camel blanket
but you are mine.
I have you to rear on a torn old mat.
Someone would like to have you as her child
but you are mine.

Silly Song

Federico Garcia Lorca
(Spain)

Mama,
I wish I were silver.

Son,
You'd be very cold.

Mama,
I wish I were water.

Son,
You'd be very cold.

Mama,
Embroider me on your pillow.

That, yes!
Right away!

Snap. Shots

Labi Siffre *(Nigeria/England)*

the first time i saw
my mum take her teeth out
i thought it was wonderful
must have been five
and i tried and i tried
but i couldn't get my teeth
to slippin' and slide out
no way could i capture
the click an' no doubt
as she took her teeth out
the matter o' fact
as she clacked 'er teeth back

•

it's unfair
that i have to wear
his old trunks
un-sleek
unlike any others on this beach
mum-made of maroon
coloured wool waterlogged
heavy with blackpool
couldn't swim if i could
inadequate dignity
one paddle backing
slack elasticity

•

twenty feet up
unassailable
never go back
and they'll never know where
anyway they don't care about me
so i'm staying forever so there
right here in this tree
that'll teach 'em a lesson
for mistreating me
i wonder
if Mum's made a cake
for tea
•

over the hills and far away
to once upon a faerie tale
of fabulous friends in fun pretendings
ever after
happy endings

Return Safely

Traditional (*Ethiopia*)

Come, come, mother of the child,
Without being pricked by the thorn,
Without being hit by the stumbling block,
Without being eaten by the hyena.

What Jenny Knows

Jackie Kay *(Nigeria /Scotland)*

'I didn't come out my mummy's tummy.
No I didn't,' I says to my pal Jenny.
But Jenny says, 'you must have.
How come?' And I replies,

'I just didn't. Get it. I didn't.'
'Everybody does' says Jenny,
who is fastly becoming an enemy.
'Rubbish,' I say. 'My mummy got me.

She picked me. She collected me.
I was in a supermarket,
on the shelf and she took me off it.'
'Nonsense,' says Jenny. 'Lies.'

'Are you calling me a liar?'
I'm getting angry. It's not funny.
'No, but you have a tendency'
(a word from her aunty, probably)

'To make things up.'
'Look. I'm speaking the Truth.'
I say, 'Cross my heart.'
'Don't hope to die,' shouts Jenny.

Awful superstitious, so she is.
'I'm adopted,' I says, 'adopted.'
'I know That!' says Jenny,
'But you still came out

Somebody's tummy. Somebody
had to have you. Didn't they?'
'Not my mummy. Not my mummy,' I says.
'Shut your face. Shut your face.'

Grown -up Blues

Terry Kee *(Singapore)*

Mother used to come when I was sick,
give me a thermometer to check my fever,
make me swallow orange aspirins,
(the ones for kids)
and tuck me in bed.

Dad used to come when I was sick
feel my forehead,
and ask if my chest hurt,
and tell me to lie down when I already was

Nobody comes now when I'm sick.
I have to feel my own forehead,
take my own temperature,
and swallow two white aspirins,
(the ones for adults).

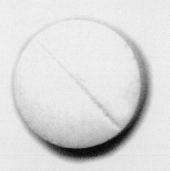

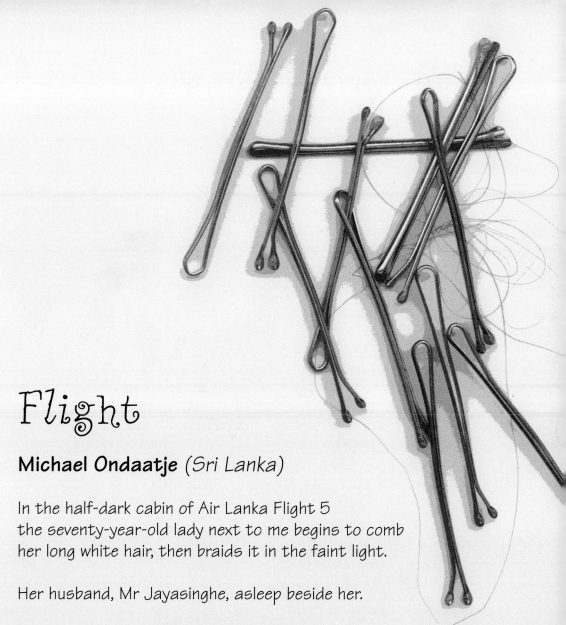

Flight

Michael Ondaatje (Sri Lanka)

In the half-dark cabin of Air Lanka Flight 5
the seventy-year-old lady next to me begins to comb
her long white hair, then braids it in the faint light.

Her husband, Mr Jayasinghe, asleep beside her.

Pins in her mouth. She rolls her hair,
curls it into a bun, like my mother's.

Two hours before reaching Katunayake airport.

An Old Woman

Arun Kolatkar (India)

An old woman grabs
hold of your sleeve
and tags along.

She wants a fifty paise coin.
She says she will take you
to the horseshoe shrine.

You've seen it already.
She hobbles along anyway
and tightens her grip on your shirt.

She won't let you go.
You know how old women are.
They stick to you like burr.

You turn around and face her
with an air of finality.
You want to end the farce.

When you hear her say,
'What else can an old woman do
on hills as wretched as these?'

You look right at the sky.
Clear through the bullet holes
she has for her eyes.

And as you look on,
the cracks that begin around her eyes
spread beyond her skin.

And the hills crack.
And the temples crack.
And the sky falls

with a plateglass clatter
around the shatterproof crone
who stands alone.

And you are reduced
to so much small change
in her hand.

A Proud Old Man (Granpa)

Paul Chidyausiku (*Zimbabwe*)

They say they are healthier
  than me,
Though they can't walk to the
  end of a mile.
At their age I walked forty at night
  to wage battle at dawn.
They think they are healthier
  than me.
If their socks get wet they
  catch cold,
When my sockless feet got wet,
  I never sneezed,
But they still think that they are
  healthier than me.
On a soft mattress over a spring
  bed
They still have to take a sleeping
  pill.
But I, with reeds cutting into my
  ribs
My head resting on a piece of
  wood,
I sleep like a baby and snore.

Jade

Janet S Wong (America/China/Korea)

Why do you wear your jade, GongGong?

Look. I tell you.
Old people bone
very crispy.
Break so easy.

Old people fall down
all the time.
Broken bone
be too bad.

Good piece jade
protect you someday.
Fall down,
Jade broken. You okay.

How do you know if your jade is good?

Shiny. Green.
Colour deep.
Good health in you
made good jade, see?

Sick, jade
look dull. Dead. White.
Your jade young, green.
You all right.

Way-Out Mum
Way-Out Dad

John Agard (Guyana)

Mum dyes her hair incandescent green
and paints her nails
a shade of midnight blue.

Dad wears a ponytail, listens to Cream
and goes on about a book
called The Tao Of Pooh.

What do you do when your parents are so liberal
they pinch your rap and heavy metal
and don't mind a nosering or tattoo?

It embarrasses me to tell,
but when their bedroom gives off that incense smell,
I know - I just know - they're smooching
and carrying on to a small Tibetan bell.

Oh what do you do with a mum and dad
who're so cool, streetwise and hip to the scene,
they make me feel like a has-been
and I'm only fourteen.

They've given me nothing
against which I can rebel.
Just to annoy them I'll grow up
sweet and straight as an angel.

Brown Honey in Broomwheat Tea

Joyce Carol Thomas (Africa/America)

My mother says I am
Brown honey in broomwheat tea
My father calls me the sweetwater
     of his days
Yet they warn
There are those who
Have brewed a
Bitter potion for
Children kissed long by the sun
Therefore I approach
The cup slowly
But first I ask
Who has set this table

We're All In The Telephone Book

Langston Hughes (Africa/America)

We're all in the telephone book,
Folks from everywhere on earth -
Anderson to Zabowski,
It's a record of America's worth.

We're all in the telephone book.
There's no priority -
A millionaire like Rockefeller
Is likely to be behind me.

For generations men have dreamed
Of nations united as one.
Just look in your telephone book
To see where that dream's begun.

When Washington crossed the Delaware
And the pillars of tyranny shook,
He started the list of democracy
That's America's telephone book.

All Mixed Up

Janet S Wong (America/China/Korea)

What does multicultural mean?

Stuck in the middle
in between
all kinds of food
and clothes
and talk?
Listening to bamboo flutes
play rock?
Turning tortillas
over the stove,
burning the tips
of chopsticks?

Why does my teacher love that word?
Is it something she ate -
or something she heard?
Loud drums
beating in the park?
Does she call me
multicultural
because my skin is
dark?

Just Like Me

Lawan Mitchell *(Africa/America)*
Black describes me.
My moods, my personality.
Black is a colour that everyone likes.
Black is subtle,
Not too flashy, not too boring.
Black is power, authority.
Black moves like air.
Close your eyes, it's everywhere.
Black is nonchalant.
Black's carefree.
Nothing phases this colour.
Black's hard as steel.

Black is my best friend.
Because we're just alike,
Plain, basic, understated,
Unlike a red or orange or yellow.
We don't brighten up a room.
We bring a coolness
That can't be produced by another.
Stone-faced is our expression.
Relaxed is our mood,
Our state of mind.
We stand alone,
But we can mix
With all people, all colours.

The Kids in School With Me

Langston Hughes (Africa/America)

When I studied my A-B-C's
And learned arithmetic,
I also learned in public school
What makes America tick:

The kid in front
And the kid behind
And the kid across the aisle,
The Italian kid
And the Polish kid
And the girl with the Irish smile,
The coloured kid
And the Spanish kid
And the Russian kid my size,
The Jewish kid
And the Grecian kid
And the girl with the Chinese eyes -
We were a regular Noah's ark,
Every race beneath the sun,
But our motto for graduation was:
One for All and All for One!
The kid in front
And the kid behind
And the kid across from me -
Just American kids together -
The kids in school with me.

No Problem

Benjamin Zephaniah (Jamaica/England)

I am not de problem
But I bare de brunt
Of silly playground taunts
An racist stunts,
I am not de problem
I am a born academic
But dey got me on de run
Now I am branded athletic,
I am not de problem
If yu give I a chance
I can teach yu of Timbuktu
I can do more dan dance,
I am not de problem
I greet yu wid a smile
Yu put me in a pigeon hole
But I am versatile.

These conditions may affect me
As I get older,
An I am positively sure
I hav no chips on me shoulders,
Black is not de problem
Mother country get it right,
An juss fe de record,
Sum of me best friends are white.

Neckgrip

John Siddique (England)

after the funeral
i found a box of photos

my mum had only ever shown me
old polaroids my dad had took
and her wedding album
                    full of the few
                    guests & had-to-be-there's

ie. those who kept their thoughts
about a black marrying a white woman,
behind their own curtains

you might call it the presence of duty

there are 3 photos in the box
all of them portraits
taken at some local photographer's studio

the props of the 50's, almost victoriana
and my father in his best suit
his neck and back rigid
in one he is holding a briefcase
in another he is pictured with a radio
in the last photograph, it is just him
standing against a dark curtained background
in his sharpest clothes:
all poses of affluence to be sent home
to give the impression of success

at home i remember
my mum telling me
about having to work 12, 14 hours in the shop
and the scraps she had to make meals with

Sugar cane

Faustin Charles (*Trinidad*)

The succulent flower bleeds molasses,
as its slender, sweet stalks bend,
beheaded in the breeze.

The green fields convulse golden sugar,
tossing the rain aside,
out-growing the sun,
and carving faces
in the sun-sliced panorama.

The reapers come at noon,
riding the cutlass-whip;
their saliva sweetens everything
in the boiling season.

Each stem is a flashing arrow,
swift in the harvest.

Cane is sweet sweat slain;
cane is labour, unrecognized, lost
and unrecovered;
sugar is the sweet swollen pain of the years;
sugar is slavery's immovable stain;
cane is water lying down,
and water standing up.

Cane is a slaver;
cane is bitter,
very bitter,
in the sweet blood of life.

Africa

David Diop (Senegal)

Africa my Africa
Africa of proud warriors in ancestral savannahs
Africa of whom my grandmother sings
On the banks of the distant river
I have never known you
But your blood flows in my veins
Your beautiful black blood that irrigates the fields
The blood of your sweat
The sweat of your work
The work of your slavery
The slavery of your children
Africa tell me Africa
Is this you this back that is bent
This back that breaks under the weight of humiliation
This back trembling with red scars
And saying yes to the whip under the midday sun
But a grave voice answers me
Impetuous son that tree young and strong
That tree there
In splendid loneliness amidst white and faded flowers
That is Africa your Africa
That grows again patiently obstinately
And its fruit gradually acquires
The bitter taste of liberty.

Telephone Conversation

Wole Soyinka *(Nigeria)*

The price seemed reasonable, location
Indifferent. The landlady swore she lived
Off premises. Nothing remained
But self-confession. 'Madam,' I warned,
'I hate a wasted journey - I am African.'
Silence. Silenced transmission of
Pressurized good-breeding. Voice, when it came,
Lipstick-coated, long gold-rolled
Cigarette-holder pipped. Caught I was, foully.
'HOW DARK?' – I had not misheard –'ARE YOU LIGHT
OR VERY DARK?' Button B. Button A. Stench
Of rancid breath of public hide-and-speak.
Red booth. Red pillar box. Red double-tiered
Omnibus squelching tar. It was real! Shamed
By ill-mannered silence, surrender
Pushed dumbfounded to beg simplification.
Considerate she was, varying the emphasis -
'ARE YOU DARK? OR VERY LIGHT?' Revelation came.
'You mean - like plain or milk chocolate?'
Her assent was clinical, crushing in its light
Impersonality. Rapidly, wave-length adjusted,
I chose. 'West African sepia' - and as an afterthought,
'Down in my passport.' Silence for spectroscopic
Flight of fancy, till truthfulness clanged her accent

Hard on the mouthpiece. 'WHAT'S THAT?' conceding
'DON'T KNOW WHAT THAT IS.' 'Like brunette.'
'THAT'S DARK, ISN'T IT?' 'Not altogether.
Facially, I am brunette, but madam, you should see
The rest of me. Palm of my hand, soles of my feet
Are a peroxide blonde. Friction, caused -
Foolishly madam - by sitting down, has turned
My bottom raven black - One moment, madam!' - sensing
Her receiver rearing on the thunderclap
About my ears - 'Madam,' I pleaded, 'wouldn't you rather
See for yourself?'

Men in Chains

Oswald Mbuyiseni Mtshali (South Africa)

The train stopped
at a country station,

Through sleep curtained eyes
I peered through the frosty window,
and saw six men:
men shorn
of all human honour
like sheep after shearing,
bleating at the blistering wind,
'Go away! Cold wind! Go away!
Can't you see we are naked?'

They hobbled into the train
on bare feet,
wrists handcuffed,
ankles manacled
with steel rings like cattle at the abbatoirs
shying away from the trapdoor.

One man with a head
shaven clean as a potato
whispered to the rising sun,
a red eye wiped by a tattered
handkerchief of clouds,
'Oh! Dear Sun!
Won't you warm my heart
with hope?'
The train went on its way to nowhere.

Two Buckets

Stanley Mogoba (South Africa)

A sleepy voice
from the confined space:
'Beware of the bucket
Move to the left;
        sleep there.
Any false move,
You fall into a lavatory bucket,
Or into drinking water next to it.'

In this startled manner,
I made my entry
Into a dark world,
Where thousands of men
Pine and are forgotten.

Cold

Dennis Brutus *(Zimbabwe)*

the clammy cement
sucks our naked feet

a rheumy yellow bulb
lights a damp grey wall

the stubbled grass
wet with three o'clock dew
is black with glittery edges;

we sit on the concrete,
stuff with our fingers
the sugarless pap
into our mouths

then labour erect;

form lines;

steel ourselves into fortitude
or accept an image of ourselves
numb with resigned acceptance;

the grizzled senior warder comments:
'Things like these
I have no time for;

they are worse than rats;
you can only shoot them.'

Overhead
the large frosty glitter of the stars
the Southern Cross flowering low;

the chains on our ankles
and wrists
that pair us together
jangle

glitter.

We begin to move
        awkwardly.

(Colesberg: en route to Robben Island)

When The Indians

William Eastlake (American)

When the Indians
Sold
New York
For a handsome
Sum of
Glass beads,
They scouted west
And crossed
What is now called
The Mississippi,
Travelling west
On what is now called
Route 66
Until they arrived at
What is now called
California.
They decided to
Sell this too
For what is now
Called money,
But the whites
Took it with
What is now called
Guns.

Alabama

Khe-Tha-A-Hi (Eagle Wing) *(Native American)*

My brethren,
among the legends of my people
it is told how a chief,
leading the remnant of his people,
crossed a great river,
and striking his tipi-stake upon the ground,
exclaimed, 'A-la-ba-ma!'
This in our language means
'Here we may rest!'
But he saw not the future.
The white man came:
he and his people could not rest there;
they were driven out,
and in a dark swamp
they were thrust down into the slime
and killed.
The word he so sadly spoke
has given a name to one of the white man's states.
There is no spot under those stars
that now smile upon us,
where the Indian can plant his foot
and sigh 'A-la-ba-ma!'

Canadian Indian Place Names

Meguido Zola (Canada)

Bella Bella, Bella Coola,
Athabaska, Iroquois;
Mesilinka, Osilinka,
Mississauga, Missisquois.
Chippewa, Chippawa,
Nottawasaga;
Malagash, Matchedash,
Shubenacadie;
Couchiching, Nipissing,
Scubenacadie.
Shickshock
Yahk
Quaw!

Folding the Sheets

Rosemary Dobson (Australia)

You and I will fold the sheets
Advancing towards each other
From Burma, from Lapland.

From India where the sheets have been washed in the river
And pounded upon stones:
Together we will match the corners.

From China where women on either side of the river
Have washed their pale cloth in the White Stone Shallows
'Under the shining moon'.

We meet as though in the formal steps of a dance
To fold the sheets together, put them to air
In wind, in sun over bushes, or by the fire.

We stretch and pull from one side and then the other -
Your turn. Now mine.
We fold them and put them away until they are needed.

A wish for all people when they lie down to sleep -
Smooth linen, cool cotton, the fragrance and stir of herbs
And the faint but perceptible scent of sweet clear water.

The Train Dogs

Pauline Johnson (Canada)

Out of the night and the north;
      Savage of breed and of bone,
Shaggy and swift comes the yelping band,
Freighters of fur from the voiceless land
      That sleeps in the Arctic zone.

Laden with skins from the north,
      Beaver and bear and raccoon,
Marten and mink from the polar belts,
Otter and ermine and sable pelts -
      The spoils of the hunter's moon.

Out of the night and the north,
      Sinewy, fearless and fleet,
Urging the pack through the pathless snow,
The Indian driver, calling low,
      Follows with moccasined feet.

Ships of the night and the north,
      Freighters on prairies and plains,
Carrying cargoes from field and flood
They scent the trail through their wild red blood,
      The wolfish blood in their veins.

The Wind Has Wings

Traditional *(Inuit)*

Nunaptigne –In our land - ahe, ahe, ee, ee, iee –
The wind has wings, winter and summer.
It comes by night and it comes by day,
And children must fear it - ahe, ahe, ee, ee, iee.
In our land the nights are long,
And the spirits like to roam in the dark.
I've seen their faces, I've seen their eyes.
They are like ravens, hovering over the dead,
Their dark wings forming long shadows,
And children must fear them - ahe, ahe, ee, ee, iee.

The Thunder is a Great Dragon

Traditional *(Mongolia)*

The thunder is a great dragon that lives in the water
and flies in the air.
He carries two stones.
When he strikes them together,
the lightning flashes and the thunder roars.
The dragon pursues the spirits of evil,
and wherever he finds them,
he slays them.
The evil spirits hide in the trees,
and the dragon destroys them.

Prayer

C P Cavafy (Greece)

A sailor drowned in the sea's depths.
Unaware, his mother goes and lights
a tall candle before the ikon of our Lady,
praying that he'll come back quickly, that
     the weather may be good -
her ear cocked always to the wind.
While she prays and supplicates,
the ikon listens, solemn, sad,
knowing the son she waits for never will
come back.

The Storm

Ashok B Raha (India)

Without warning a snake of black
cloud rises in the sky.
It hisses as it runs and spreads its hood.
The moon goes out, the mountain is dark.
Far away is heard the shout of the demon.

Up rushes the storm a moment after
Rattling an iron chain in its teeth
The mountain suddenly lifts its
Trunk to the heavens
And the lake roars like a wild beast.

Problems with Hurricanes

Victor Hernandez Cruz (Puerto Rico)

A campesino looked at the air
And told me:
With hurricanes it's not the wind
or the noise or the water.
I'll tell you he said:

it's the mangoes, avocados
Green plantains and bananas
flying into town like projectiles.
How would your family
feel if they had to tell
The generations that you
got killed by a flying
Banana?

Death by drowning has honour
If the wind picked you up
and slammed you
Against a mountain boulder
This would not carry shame
But
to suffer a mango smashing
Your skull
or a plantain hitting your
Temple at 70 miles per hour
is the ultimate disgrace.

The campesino takes off his hat -
As a sign of respect
towards the fury of the wind
And says:
Don't worry about the noise
Don't worry about the water
Don't worry about the wind -
If you are going out
beware of mangoes
And all such beautiful
sweet things.

Good Food Guide

Jackie Kay (Nigeria/Scotland)

I wouldn't touch a hamburger
but I crave guacamole,
gazpacho and water melon.
I wouldn't go near fried bread,
but I would go bananas
for a blueberry pancake.
A glass of milk tastes very sly,
but sweet lassi would go down nicely.

There's things I wouldn't consider:
an English breakfast with ketchup.
But I'd stand up and shout
please, or go down on my knees
for ackee and cornbread,
baba ghanoush, ratatouille,
couscous, tagliatelle.
Don't give me custard and jelly,
give me sweet potato pie,
or tiramisu or Turkish delight.

There are words that taste
better than chocolate
words that roll and melt
words that can dip and swirl and sigh
words that make my mouth water
words that I can relish and suck and savour.

Go for the tasty, delicious words -
sag aloo, gadoh gadoh.
Don't give me a boring old plum.
Try me with a dim sum.
I'll eat my words.

Knoxville, Tennessee

Nikki Giovanni *(Africa/America)*

I always like summer
best
you can eat fresh corn
from daddy's garden
and okra
and greens
and cabbage
and lots of
barbecue
and buttermilk
and homemade ice-cream
at the church picnic
and listen to
gospel music
outside
at the church
homecoming
and go to the mountain with
your grandmother
and go barefooted
and be warm
all the time
not only when you go to bed
and sleep

Drinking Water-Coconut

Grace Nichols (*Guyana*)

Feeling thirsty
feeling hot
nothing to cool you down
like a water-coconut

With a flick of her cutlass
market-lady will hand you one -
a sweet little hole brimming at the top
when you put it to yuh head
you wouldn't want it to stop

Then you'll be wondering
if there's jelly inside
ask market-lady she wouldn't mind
she'll flick the big nut right open for you
she'll flick you a coconut spoon
to scoop with too

Feeling thirsty
feeling hot
the best thing to spend yuh money on
is a water-coconut

Munchausen in Alberta

Elizabeth Brewster (Canada)

Our first winter in the settlement,
the old man said,
January was so cold
the flames in the lamp froze.
The women picked them like strawberries
and gave them to the children to eat.

That's the only time
I was ever a fire-eater.

The Rich Eat Three Full Meals

Nguyen Binh Khiem *(Vietnam)*

The rich eat three full meals, the poor two small bowls,
But peace is what matters.
Thirsty, I drink sweet plum tea;
Warm, I lie in the shade, in the breeze;
My paintings are mountains and rivers all around me,
My damask, embroidered, the grass.
I rest at night, rest easy,
Am awake with the sun
And enjoying Heaven's heaped-up favours.

Gold

Ferenc Juhasz *(Hungary)*

The woman touches her bun
of thinning hair. She laughs,
and drops a spoon and a hunk of bread
in their reaching, grubby hands.
Like roses divining water
the circle of thin red necks
leans over the steaming plates;
red noses bloom in the savoury mist.

The stars of their eyes shine
like ten worlds lost in their own light.
In the soup, slowly circling
swim golden onion rings.

Black Widow

Valerie Bloom *(Trinidad)*

I hear there's a spider wot eats 'er 'usband
I think that's well bad,
I'm glad I'm not a spider,
I wouldn't like mum to eat dad.

Blue Cheese, Raw Fish And Olives

Salena Saliva Godden (England)

When I grow up I will actually like olives,
And understand the need for an early bed,
And why I don't have to finish the bottle,
And why poems don't have to rhyme –
Red,
Lipstick will suit and stay on my lips,
And I will walk delicately, elegant in high heels,
I will have credit cards and generously tip,
Wonder if the world is getting younger and know how that feels.

'Excuse me, Madame Lady' strangers will say,
Offering me something nice, perhaps a cake slice,
And I will reply in a grown up lady type way,
'Oh! No thankyou, that will surely suffice.'
When I grow up, I will actually like olives,
And while putting cool cucumbers on my tired eyes,
I will eat stuffed black ones truly believing they taste good,
Like blue cheese, raw fish and all other grown up lies.

The Kangaroo

Leon Gellert *(Australia)*

The very best Australian stew
always includes a kangaroo.
So if one happens to be shot,
just try it when you make a pot.
Lest you become a laughing-stock it
May be as well to search its pocket
For odds and ends that it may hold;-
Like lozenges (against a cold) -
Or rubber bands or bits of string -
Or bottle tops or anything
That filled the wretched creature's needs
From rolls of braid to coloured beads.
Such adjuncts (as the gourmet has it)
Possess no culinary asset.

Cat

Edward Kamau Brathwaite   (Caribbean)

To plan plan to create to have
whiskers cool carat silver ready and curved
bristling

to plan plan to create to have
eyes green doors that dilate greenest
pouncers

to be ready rubber ball ready
feet bouncers cool fluid in
tension

to be steady steady claws all
attention to wait wait and create
pouncing

to be a cat eeling through alleys
slipping through windows of odours
to feel swiftness slowly

to halt at the gate hearing
unlocking whispers paper feet wrapping
potatoes and papers

to hear nicely mice spider feet
scratching great horny nails
catching a fire flies wire legs etch-
ing yet stretching beyond this arch
untriumphant lazily rubb-
ing the soft fur of home

Pusscat

Anna Akhmatova (Russia)

Pusscat, watch out, an embroidered owl
Scowls from a pillow on the bed,
Grey Miss Pusscat, please don't growl,
Granddad will hear what you just said.
Nanny, this candle isn't lit,
Mice can nibble me if they try.
That dratted owl, I'm afraid of it,
Who embroidered him and why?

Egrets

Judith Wright *(Australia)*

Once as I travelled through a quiet evening,
I saw a pool, jet-black and mirror-still.
Beyond, the slender paperbarks stood crowding;
each on its own white image looked its fill,
and nothing moved but thirty egrets wading -
thirty egrets in a quiet evening.

Once in a lifetime, lovely past believing,
your lucky eyes may light on such a pool.
As though for many years I had been waiting,
I watched in silence, till my heart was full
of clear dark water, and white trees unmoved,
and, whiter yet, those thirty egrets wading.

St Francis And The Birds

Seamus Heaney *(Ireland)*

When Francis preached love to the birds
They listened, fluttered, throttled up
Into the blue like a flock of words

Released for fun from his holy lips,
Then wheeled back, whirred about his head,
Pirouetted on brothers' capes.

Danced on the wing, for sheer joy played
And sang, like images took flight.
Which was the best poem Francis made,
His argument true, his tone light.

I Watched An Eagle Soar

Virginia Driving Hawk Sneve (Native American)

Grandmother,
I watched an eagle soar
high in the sky
until a cloud covered him up.
Grandmother,
I still saw the eagle
behind my eyes.

Be A Butterfly

Grace Nichols (Guyana)

Don't be a kyatta-pilla
Be a butterfly
old preacher screamed
to illustrate his sermon
of Jesus and the higher life

rivulets of well-earned
sweat sliding down
his muscly mahogany face
in the half-empty school church
we sat shaking with muffling
laughter
watching our mother trying to save
herself from joining the wave

only our father remaining poker face
and afterwards we always went home to
split peas Sunday soup
with dumplings, fufu and pigtail

Don't be a kyatta-pilla
Be a butterfly
Be a butterfly

That was de life preacher
and you was right

The Spider And The Fly

Mohammed Iqbal (Pakistan)

The spider said to the fly:
'Do look in when you come by.
It will be an honour.
I have a new home, new decor;
See the staircase and the curtains,
And the walls are hung with mirrors.'
The fly hesitated: 'I don't know
I haven't seen anyone going up the stairs
That came down again.' The spider
Then resorted to flattery:
'You are looking absolutely lovely;
Your eyes sparkle like sequins,
and that glittering dress!
I must say you are always busy
washing yourself and humming
As you fly that soothing tune.'
The fly winged past, flattered
That she had a new admirer.
'All right' she said and entered the web.

i Hate Flies

Labi Siffre (Nigeria/England)

I hate flies
really hate 'em
loathe their filthy, disease carrying habits

tasting your food with their feet
vomiting
then sucking the vomit back up
with some of your food
mixed in
I kill 'em whenever I can

sprays, supplements, rolled up newspapers,
paperback latest sci-fi thriller
but a hand towel is best
and for distance track-suit
bottoms held by the ankles

and now you say
they pollinate more flowers than bees do
THWACK!!

That's something I'll have to
think about

A Dragonfly In The Sun

Zulfikar Ghose (Pakistan/England)

The afternoon's light is caught
in the dragonfly's wings where
transparency permits no reflections
and yet will not give free passage
to the sun, preserving the surface
brightness of delicate webbing
as a fragile brilliance of gleaming
points which made the wings nearly
invisible and the diagonal markings appear
as tiny irradiations of very faint
pink and blue when the dragonfly
darts up against the sun as if it
plucked colours from the air
and immediately discarded them:
this is the moment of intensity,
of the afternoon's light gathering
in the garden in a brief flickering
of a dragonfly's wings just above
the red blossoms of the pomegranate.

Reflected

Issa (Japan)

Reflected
in the dragonfly's eye -
mountains.

The Fairy Horse

Traditional *(Serbia)*

A girl threw an apple to a cloud,
And the cloud kept the apple.
The girl prayed to all the clouds:
Brother clouds, give me back my golden apple.
The guests have arrived:
My mother's brothers and my uncles.
Their horses are wild like mountain fairies.
When they tread the dust
The dust doesn't rise.
When they tread on water,
Their hooves don't get wet.

Dozing On Horseback

Basho *(Japan)*

Dozing on horseback,
smoke from tea-fires
drifts to the moon.

My Apologies

Buland Al-Haidari   (Iraq)

My apologies, my honoured guests,
The newsreader lied in his last bulletin:
There is no sea in Baghdad
Nor pearls
Not even an island,
And everything Sinbad said
About the queens of the jinn
About the ruby and coral islands
About the thousand thousands flowing from the sultan's hand
Is a myth born in the summer heat
      Of my small town
In the burnt-up shadows of the midday sun
In the silent nights of the exiled stars.
We used to have
A sea, shells, pearls
      And a polished moon
And fishermen returning in the evening;

We used to have,
Said the newsreader's last bulletin,
An innocent, dream paradise;
For we, my honoured guests,
Lie to be born again,
Lie to stretch in our long history
The myth told by Sinbad -
We used to have
A sea, shells, pearls
        And the hour of birth.

My apologies, my honoured guests,
The newsreader lied in his last bulletin:
There is no sea in Baghdad
Nor pearls
Not even an island.

Muliebrity

Sujata Bhatt *(India/America)*

I have thought so much about the girl
who gathered cow-dung in a wide, round basket
along the main road passing by our house
and the Radhavallabh temple in Maninagar.
I have thought so much about the way she
moved her hands and her waist
and the smell of cow-dung and road-dust and wet canna lilies,
the smell of monkey breath and freshly washed clothes
and the dust from crows' wings which smells different -
and again the smell of cow-dung as the girl scoops
it up, all these smells surrounding me separately
and simultaneously - I have thought so much
but have been unwilling to use her for a metaphor,
for a nice image - but most of all unwilling
to forget her or to explain to anyone the greatness
and the power glistening through her cheekbones
each time she found a particularly promising
mound of dung

The Railway Clerk

Nissim Ezekial *(India)*

It isn't my fault.
I do what I'm told
but still I am blamed.
This year, my leave application
was twice refused.
Every day there is so much work
and I don't get overtime.
My wife is always asking for more money.
Money, money, where to get money?
My job is such, no one is giving bribe,
while other clerks are in fortunate position,
and no promotion even because I am not graduate.

I wish I was bird.

I am never neglecting my responsibility,
I am discharging it properly,
I am doing my duty,
but who is appreciating?
Nobody, I am telling you.

My desk is too small,
the fan is not repaired for two months,
three months.
I am living far off in Borivli,
my children are neglecting studies,
how long this can go on?

Schoolmaster

Yevgeny Yevtushenko (Russia)

The window gives onto the white trees.
The master looks out of it at the trees,
for a long time, he looks for a long time
out through the window at the trees,
breaking his chalk slowly in one hand.
And it's only the rules of long division.
And he's forgotten the rules of long division.
Imagine not remembering long division!
A mistake on the blackboard, a mistake.

We watch him with a different attention
needing no one to hint to us about it,
there's more than difference in this attention.
The schoolmaster's wife has gone away,
we do not know where she has gone to,
we do not know why she has gone,
what we know is his wife has gone away.

His clothes are neither new nor in the fashion;
wearing the suit which he always wears
and which is neither new nor in the fashion
the master goes downstairs to the cloakroom.
He fumbles in his pocket for a ticket.
'What's the matter? Where is that ticket?
Perhaps I never picked up my ticket.
Where is the thing?' Rubbing his forehead.

'Oh, here it is. I'm getting old
Don't argue auntie dear, I'm getting old.
You can't do much about getting old.'
We hear the door below creaking behind him.
The window gives onto the white trees.
The trees there are high and wonderful,
but they are not why we are looking out.
We look in silence at the schoolmaster.

He has a bent back and clumsy walk,
he moves without defences, clumsily,
worn out I ought to have said, clumsily.
Snow falling on him softly through the silence
turns him to white under the white trees.
A little longer will make him so white
we shall not see him on the whitened trees.

ыходит в белые деревья.

ссор долго смотрит на деревья.

ь долго смотрит на деревья

долго мел крошит в руке.

о просто —

правила деленья!

был их —

Clowns

Miroslav Holub (Czechoslovakia)

Where do clowns go,
what do clowns eat,
where do clowns sleep,

what do clowns do,
when nobody,
just nobody laughs
any more,
Mummy?

The Man On The Desert Island (1)

Gerda Mayer (Czechoslovakia/England)

The man on the desert island
Has forgotten the ways of people,
His stories are all of himself.
Day in, day out of time
He communes with himself and sends
Messages in green bottles:
Help me, they say, I am
Cast up and far from home.
Each day he goes to watch
The horizon for ships.
Nothing reaches his shore
Except corked green bottles.

A Song For England

Andrew Salkey *(Jamaica)*

An a so de rain a-fall
An a so de snow a-rain

An a so de fog a-fall
An a so de sun a-fail

An a so de seasons mix
An a so de bag-o-tricks

But a so me understan
De misery o de Englishman.

Thought For Monday

Benjamin Zephaniah *(Jamaica/England)*

Why do people
Complain about Mondays,
Why do
People have
Monday morning blues
And that Monday morning feeling?
Monday is like any other day.

I think
People who suffer Monday morning blues
Read too many Sunday papers.

Poetics

Benjamin Zephaniah *(Jamaica/England)*

There's a poem on your face
There's a poem in the sky
There's a poem in outta space
There are poems passing by,
There are poems in your dreams
There are poems in your head
Sometimes I cannot get to sleep
Cause there are poems in me bed.

There are poems in me tea
There are poems on me toast
I have found much poetry
In the place I love the most,
There's a poem right in front of you
Get to know its rhyme,
If you are not sure what to do
Just call it poem time.

There's a poem in me shoes
There's a poem in me shirt
When the poem meets the blues
It can really, really hurt,
Other poems make you grin
When they dribble off your chin
Some poems think they are great
So they like to make you . . .

                    Wait
I see poems in your teeth
I see poems in me cat
I hear poems underneath
Going rata tat tat tat,
This one had not finished yet
It keeps coming on the beat
It is soggy and it's wet
But it's also very sweet.

There are poems for the ear
There are poems for the page
Some poems are not quite clear
but they get better with age,
There are poems for the hip
There are poems for the hop
Everything is poetic

Poetry will never stop.

There are poems on your fingers
There's a poem on your nose
If you give it time to linger
It will grow and grow and grow,
There's a poem in you beautiful
Can't you see it
It's right
                    There,
I think it's so incredible
There are poems
Everywhere.

Author Index

Acknowledgements

Adonis: 'The Bird', from *Modern Poetry of the Arab World*, published in 1986 by Penguin Books Ltd. By permission of Abdullah al-Udhari.

John Agard: 'Way-Out Mum, Way-Out Dad'. By kind permission of John Agard, from *Get Back Pimple*, published in 1996 by Viking Press.

Sujata Bhatt: 'Muliebrity', from *Brunziem*, published by Carcanet Press Ltd. By permission of Carcanet Press Ltd.

Valerie Bloom: 'Black Widow' and 'Frost', published by Bloomsbury Publishing plc.

George Mackay Brown: 'The Guardians', from *Travellers*, published by John Murray (Publishers) Ltd. By permission of John Murray (Publishers) Ltd.

C.P. Cavafy: 'Prayer', from *Collected Poems* by C.P.Cavafy, the estate of C.P.Cavafy, the translators Edmund Keeley and Philip Sherrard and Hogarth Press as publisher. Used by permission of the Random House Group Limited.

Imtiaz Dharker: 'Outline' and 'Prayer', from *Postcards from god*. Published in 1997 by Bloodaxe Books. By permission of Bloodaxe Books.

David Diop: 'Africa', from *The Penguin Book of Modern African Poetry*, edited by Gerald Moore and Ulli Beier, first published as *Modern Poetry From Africa*, 1963 (Penguin Books, 1984) copyright © Gerald Moore and Ulli Beier, 1963, 1968, 1984. By permission of Penguin Books Ltd.

Sergei Esenin: 'Night', from *Confessions of a Hooligan*, published by Carcanet Press Ltd. By permission of Carcanet Press Ltd.

John Foulcher: 'Martin and the Hand Grenade', from *Light Pressure*. By permission of Harper Collins Publishers.

Buland al-Haidari: 'My Apologies', from *Modern Poetry of the Arab World*, published in 1986 by Penguin Books Ltd. By permission of Abdullah al-Udhari.

Seamus Heaney: 'St Francis and the Bird', from *Death of a Naturalist*. By permission of Faber and Faber.

Miroslav Holub: 'The Door', translated by Ian Milner, from *Poems Before and After: Collected English Translations*. Published in 1990 by Bloodaxe Books. By permission of Bloodaxe Books.

Langston Hughes: 'The Kids in School With Me' and 'We're all in the Telephone Book', from *The Collected Poems of Langston Hughes*, published in 1995 by Random House Inc.

Jackie Kay: 'Good Food Guide', from *Three Has Gone*, published in 1994 by Penguin. 'What Jenny Knows', from *Two's Company*, published by Penguin. Both reprinted by permission of PFD on behalf of Jackie Kay.

Gerda Mayer: 'The Man on the Desert Island 1', from *Bernini's Cat*, published in 1999 by Iron Press. First published in *And* magazine, 1963. Copyright © Gerda Mayer.

Oswald Mtshali: 'Inside my Zulu Hut', from *The Penguin Book of Modern African Poetry*, edited by Gerald Moore and Ulli Beier, first published as *Modern Poetry From Africa*, 1963 (Penguin Books, 1984) copyright © Gerald Moore and Ulli Beier, 1963, 1968, 1984. By permission of Penguin Books Ltd.

Stephen Mulrine: 'The Coming of the Wee Malkies'. By permission of Stephen Mulrine.

Grace Nichols: 'Be A Butterfly', from *The Fat Black Woman's Poems*. Reproduced with permission of Curtis Brown Ltd, London, on behalf of Grace Nichols. Copyright © Grace Nichols, 1984.

Michael Ondaatje: 'Flight' and 'The First Rule of Sinhalese Architecture', published by Bloomsbury plc.

Labi Siffre: 'I Hate Flies' and 'Snap Shots', from *Nigger*. By permission of Labi Siffre, author of poetry books *Nigger*, *Blood On The Page* and *Monument* (Xavier Books).

Charles Simic: 'The Fairy Horse', from *Sheep Don't Go to School*, published in 1999 by Bloodaxe Books. By permission of Faber and Faber.

Virginia Driving Hawk Sneve: ' I Watched An Eagle Soar', copyright © Virginia Driving Hawk Sneve. From *Dancing Tepees*, published in 1989 by Oxford University Press. By permission of John Johnson Ltd.

Joyce Carol Thomas: 'Brown Honey in Broomwheat Tea', from *Brown Honey in Broomwheat Tea*, published in 1993 by Harper Collins Publishers.

R S Thomas: 'The Small Window', from *Collected Poems*. Published by Phoenix, an imprint of the Orion Publishing Group Ltd.

Janet S.Wong: 'All Mixed Up' and 'Jade'. Reprinted with the permission of Margaret K.McElderry Books, an imprint of Simon & Schuster Children's Publishing Division. From *Good Luck Gold and Other Poems* by Janet S. Wong. Copyright © 1994 Janet S.Wong.

Yevgeny Yevtushenko: 'Schoolmaster', from *Selected Poems: Yevtushenko*, translated by Robin Milner-Gulland and Peter Levi (Penguin Books, 1962) copyright © Robin Milner-Gulland and Peter Levi, 1962. By permission of Penguin Books Ltd.

Benjamin Zephaniah: 'No Problem', and 'Thought For Monday' from *Funky Chickens*, published by Viking Books. 'Poetics', from *Propa Propaganda*, published in 1999 by Bloodaxe Books. By permission of Bloodaxe Books.

Every effort has been made to trace the copyright holders but in some cases this has not proved possible. The publisher will be happy to rectify any such errors or omissions in future reprints and/or new editions.